Knowing about Internet of Things

Internet of Things made easy

By

Maren Felicity
Copyright@2022

WEB

To familiarize you with the improvement surroundings, your first program Ought to be a easy HelloWorld.

The USB connection is Used to deploy and debug your applications, and inside the HelloWorld example, it

Permits you to ship the hiya international string to your improvement computer.

Architecture of HelloWorld instance

Environment

Before writing your first application for the .Internet Micro Framework, you need

To put in a few gear and libraries, together with:

» Microsoft visual Studio 2010 or later. The loose visible Studio explicit

Model is enough. Full commercial versions also can be used, of

Four Getting started with the internet of factors

Course. For my descriptions and screenshots, i will use visible Studio

These types of software programs are loose. The above tools require home windows XP, Vista, or windows 7.

The keywords public static void specify the type of the approach;

In this example, it's public (is visible to other training), static (doesn't need an

Example of the HelloWorld class to execute the method), and void (doesn't

Return a value). Additionally, because the parentheses are empty, primary() doesn't

Expect you to pass it any arguments (gadgets or variables that might be

Stated inside the technique).

In reality, you won't name major() in your own; NETMF does it for you. When

The Netduino Plus reboots or is powered on, it appears for the primary() method

1/howdy international 5

And runs it as the entry factor of your software. This application writes the

String hey international to a debug console, e.G., the Output window of visual Studio.

Debug's Print technique writes text output at once to the development
Environment through the same delivery (connection) used for deploying

Software to the device and for debugging. At the Netduino Plus board, it

Is a USB delivery. Different development boards may additionally use a serial shipping(RS-232) or an Ethernet shipping.

Building the program

In visual Studio

Assuming you have got already installed the .Net Micro Framework SDK and

The Netduino SDK, there are a few steps you have to comply with before you can Kind in the HelloWorld application:

1. Begin visual Studio.

2. Click on file→New task....

3. Pick Micro Framework within the established Templates pane, select Netduino

Plus utility inside the center pane, and sort HelloWorld inside the call

Discipline at the lowest (see determine 1-2). Then click adequate.

4. Within the solution Explorer on the proper side, double-click on program.Cs.
A tab with the name program.Cs will open, containing some boilerplate

Software text.

5. Replace the text with the HelloWorld program from instance 1-1.

6. Select Debug→construct way to build the answer. At the bottom-left Nook of visible Studio, it need to now say "build succeeded".

Deploying to the tool

Once you have constructed the instance, you may deploy it on your hardware.

1. Inside the answer Explorer, right-click on on the HelloWorld project (just under

The textual content "solution 'HelloWorld' (1 mission)"), then pick out properties within the Menu.

2. At the left facet, click on on the .Internet Micro Framework tab, which leads to

The conversation field shown in parent 1-four. Ensure that the residences are set

Up as follows:

» Configuration: lively (Debug)

» Platform: lively (Any CPU)

» delivery: USB

» tool: select your Netduino from the drop-down listing.

3.If the tool list field says <none>, you need to plug to your Netduino Plus.
The primary time you plug it in, the driver should be installed automatically.

Its name should seem whilst you click on on the device list field.

4. To open the Output window, so one can show debug output, use the keyboard shortcut Ctrl-W, followed through O.

5. Next, select Debug→begin Debugging, and the HelloWorld software will Be despatched for your board, loaded via the .Net Micro Framework, after which

The principle technique is accomplished. The program then terminates at once.

You can see the debug output in visible Studio. The end of the output

Have to look some thing like this:

The thread '<No Name>' (0x2) has exited with code zero (0x0).

Good day international

The thread '<No Name>' (0x1) has exited with code 0 (0x0).

This system '[1] Micro Framework utility: controlled' has exited with code zero (0x0).

If a conversation field with the text "There have been deployment errors.

Keep?" appears, click on the No button. Rebuild this system.

Then plug in the USB cable again and immediately click on Debug→begin

Debugging. In some uncommon instances (usually regarding complicated

Packages), the tool appears to get without a doubt caught, and a energy cycle

Doesn't assist. In the ones instances, it could assist to erase your software from

The Netduino Plus the use of the following steps:

1. Start up the MFDeploy tool (defined in chapter 6) and ensure USB is selected.

2. Unplug your Netduino Plus, then plug it lower back in whilst protecting down the

Onboard button.

3. Release the button after which press the Erase button on the MFDeploy Tool.

WRITING TO ACTUATORS

You could now write your first absolutely embedded application. In a time-commemorated

Subculture, this program, BlinkingLed, that's the embedded equivalent Of HelloWorld, makes an LED blink.

This LED is hooked up to a popular-reason input/output (GPIO)

Pin of the microcontroller. Most microcontrollers have a number of such

GPIO pins, each of which can be configured as digital input or digital output.

A digital output is probably connected to an LED, as in our example; a digital

Input might be connected to a transfer or button.

The BlinkingLed software, contains a easy infinite loop that switches the LED on, waits for 1/2 a 2d, switches the

LED off again, waits for every other 1/2 a second, after which begins all over.

The calls to the Sleep approach within the Thread magnificence make this system

Pause for (at the least) a given quantity of milliseconds (a millisecond is

1/one thousandth of a 2d). Inside the .Net Micro Framework, the usage of Thread.Sleep

Is the satisfactory practice for waiting, as it allows the hardware to enter a lowerpower country to preserve energy.

Hardware.OutputPort. Of path, you can spell out the entire name of

The elegance each time you use it, however for the sake of clarity and

Convenience, it is frequently most appropriate to use a using directive. If you

Specify the directive using Microsoft.SPOT.Hardware; (as I did in

BlinkingLed) at the beginning of your software, you may use the short

Call OutputPort, as opposed to the whole name. I'm able to use brief names in

This ebook; please see the tables in Appendix B to discover the perfect

Namespace for every class utilized in these examples.

Note: The "SPOT" in several NETMF namespaces stands for smart

Private object technology, initially evolved for programmable

Non-public devices along with watches. The .Net Micro Framework grew out Of these activities.

Strolling the program

To run the program, create a new Netduino Plus utility mission in Visual Studio, and replace the contents of software.Cs with the code.

Digital Outputs

Inside the .Net Micro Framework, the usage of a physical pin as output is represented

By way of an output port item, which is an instance of the magnificence OutputPort.

An output port affords the technique Write that takes the target country of

The output pin as a Boolean (authentic or fake) parameter.

1 instead, these pins may be configured as virtual inputs or as virtual outputs.
Be aware: Many exceptional bright blue and white LEDs can tolerate the three.3V

GPIOs that the Netduino Plus uses. You could connect such an led to any

Of the GPIO pins: the lengthy lead (fantastic) is going to the GPIO pin, and the

Short lead (poor) is going to the board's ground pin. But, if you

Are using an LED of every other colour, notice that it prefers a lower voltage;

Therefore, you should put a 220 ohm resistor among one of the LED's

Leads (both one is good enough) and your board.

The second one parameter of the OutputPort constructor proven in instance 2-1

Indicates whether or not the LED have to first of all be switched on or off. In our case, Fake shows that it ought to be off at the start.

LightSwitch

The program LightSwitch (instance 3-1) reads the cutting-edge transfer state

Periodically and copies it to the LED. That is achieved frequently sufficient that a

Person does now not come across a postpone while she opens or closes the transfer. Delays

Of 1/tenth of a second or much less are undetectable through people; consequently, the

Loop is performed each 100 milliseconds.

Note: A value read from a sensor—in this case, the switch or button—is

Called a size or sample. The time span between two subsequent

Measurements is called the sampling length.

VIRTUAL INPUTS

For studying the transfer nation, create item switchPort of type InputPort

For the pin to which your board's transfer is attached (in this case, i use

The ONBOARD_SW1 steady to refer to the pin that's stressed to the Netduino's

Integrated switch). While an input port is created, you have to skip

Parameters in addition to the pin range: bool glitchFilter and Port.

ResistorMode resistor.

Parameter glitchFilter determines whether button presses are

Debounced—i.E., whether or not intermittent mechanical contacts are

Suppressed. In LightSwitch, it doesn't certainly count whether or not a cost is

Study that is "incorrect" temporarily; consequently, I bypass false. This will be

Distinct if the application did something crucial whenever the button

Become pressed, like launching rockets. In such a situation, you wouldn't

Want one keypress to release an entire salvo of rockets, clearly due to the fact

The button jumps up and down a piece earlier than it settles down.

To understand the resistor parameter, we want to take a look at the hardware

Of the board. The microcontroller's input pin ONBOARD_SW1 is attached to

Strength (PWR)—i.E., to the deliver voltage on the only hand—and through switch

SW1 to floor (GND), or to 0 voltage. With out resistance between

Strength and ground, it'd be uncertain what the enter pin would see when

The transfer is closed (determine three-2). Strength? Ground? Some thing in among?

Figure 3-2. Why a resistor is wanted

18 Getting started out with the internet of things

Moreover, the cutting-edge would turn out to be limitless whilst the transfer is closed—

In different phrases, you'll get a short circuit that might break the Board. These are the motives why a resistor R should be provided. It limits

The present day, prevents a short circuit, and defines whether ONBOARD_SW1

Detects a high or a low voltage. On the Netduino Plus board, this pull-up

Resistor is located among ONBOARD_SW1 and power. Determine 3-3 suggests an

Excerpt of board schematics that illustrates the situations with switch SW1 open (left) and closed (right).

Because the Netduino Plus board already provides a pull-up

resistor for

ONBOARD_SW1, the microcontroller pin doesn't need to provide extra

Resistance of its own. Consequently, the value Port.ResistorMode.Disabled

Is surpassed as a parameter to the enter port constructor.

Note: If there had been no outside pull-up resistor at the board, you would

Must bypass Port.ResistorMode.PullUp to allow the microcontroller's

Inner pull-up resistor. That is applicable in case you use one of the digital inputs

On the Netduino Plus connectors to connect an externalswitch.

Superb and poor logic

It'd be nonintuitive if an input port with transfer semantics

Returned real for an open switch, so the Netduino GPIO driver

Makes certain that switchPort.Read returns fake for an open

Switch (excessive voltage), and true for a closed transfer (low voltage).

But, be conscious that if you use other GPIO ports with switches

And pull-up resistors attached, they will return proper for open

Switches. That is due to the fact the framework can not recognize the preferred

Semantics in advance, and therefore it can't modify different ports

Than ONBOARD_SW1 for this poor logic!

The board schematics in determine 3-three are simplified because on the

Netduino, the identical transfer is used as a reset button if it's now not used as a

GPIO port, which requires extra common sense no longer shown right here. With out this

Common sense, SW1 and R could have been swapped, turning R right into a pull-down

Resistor. This would have avoided using terrible logic.

The purpose why hardware is often designed with pull-up resistors

In place of pull-down resistors is historical: in advance circuit technology

Had integrated pull-up resistors. With these days's CMOS circuits, there's no

Technical cause anymore, however the lifestyle of the usage of a mixture of superb And poor good judgment lamentably remains.

VoltageReader

Analyzing virtual inputs for buttons, switches, etc is pleasant, however from time to time you could need to examine analog inputs as properly. The VoltageReader in

Determine three-four suggests how this may be accomplished.

It polls a potentiometer each Three seconds and prints the raw cost and the corresponding voltage Cost to the debug output.

ANALOG INPUTS

A regular analog sensor interprets a few bodily phenomenon, consisting of

Temperature, right into a voltage stage. The analog/virtual converter (ADC) constructed

Into the microcontroller of the Netduino Plus can degree this voltage And flip it into an integer number.

However, we can no longer be configuring all of the linked pins to

Be analog inputs. Consider that the analog pins at the Netduino can be used

Both for preferred-reason digital I/O or for analog input. In our case, we

Will configure the pins at the two ends (A0 and A2) to be virtual outputs

Presenting three.3V on one pin and zero.0V on the opposite. Only the center pin (A1)

Could be configured to be an analog input.

Parent 3-6 shows a schematic diagram for this association of additives.

Determine three-6. Potentiometer related to three microcontroller pins

The symbol for a potentiometer seems similar to a resistor because it

Is indeed a sort of variable resistor. Relying on how you turn the

Potentiometer's knob, the resistances among pins A0 and A1 at the

One hand, and between pins A1 and A2 then again, will alternate.

POTENTIOMETER AS A VARIABLE VOLTAGE DIVIDER

With your potentiometer attached to the Netduino Plus, you have

Palms-on experience with an analog sensor. This is a good foundation for

Gaining knowledge of about extra superior sensors later on. In spite of everything, most analog

Sensors produce various voltages that the Netduino measures at certainly one of

The analog inputs, representing them as an unsigned integer fee.

Pins A0 and A2 are used as digital outputs here, forcing one in every of them to low

(fake) and the opposite to excessive (real). The Netduino Plus allows using

Pins A0 to A5 as either analog inputs, or as virtual inputs or outputs (i.E., as

GPIOs). This trick lets you use one pin as voltage (excessive corresponds to 3.3

Volt) and one as ground (zero.0 Volt).

Reading an analog input port is completed with this line:

Int rawValue = voltagePort.Study();

This yields a cost between zero and 1023. Scaling it to between zero.0 and three.Three

Volt is accomplished within the following way:

Double price = (rawValue * maxVoltage) / maxAdcValue;

We multiply the price we read (rawValue) via the maximum voltage (three.Three)

And divide it by using the maximum cost possible (1023).

Voltage Divider

A voltage divider produces an output voltage that may be a fraction of its

Enter voltage. In discern three-7, the output voltage seen at GPIO_PIN_A1

Is 3.3V * (R2 / (R1 + R2)). A potentiometer allows you to trade R2

By way of turning its knob.

Different sensors have their resistances changed via different

Physical outcomes. As an example, brightness impacts the resistance of A photo resistor.

In this component, we can see how devices may be programmed as HTTP clients,

Getting access to services at the net. The primary focus will be on Pachube,

A carrier created in particular for internet of factors programs. Your

Device(s) can ship measurements to Pachube for storage and for later

Get admission to via net browsers or other applications.

The .Net Micro Framework provides especially two utility programming

Interfaces (APIs) for implementing HTTP clients: the excessive-degree HttpWebRequest API (in namespace gadget.Net) and the low-level Socket API (in

Namespace machine). You'll learn how to paintings with either one, depending

For your application needs and available hardware resources.

Now that you have seen how to paintings with simple sensors and actuators,

It is time to take the next step in the direction of an internet of factors software.

In this bankruptcy, i can in short introduce the internet of factors, and the

Related net of things.

The net of factors is a global community of computer systems, sensors, and

Actuators connected through internet protocols.

A most basic instance is a laptop that communicates over the net with a

Small device, in which the device has a sensor connected (e.G., a temperature

Sensor), as shown in discern four-1.

Determine four-1. A laptop and a tool related via the net

The TCP/IP protocol is the key internet protocol for such communique

Situations. It allows the switch of byte streams between two computer systems

In either direction. As an instance, the usage of the TCP/IP protocol, the device in Determine four-1 might also periodically supply temperature measurements to a Software walking at the laptop.

HTTP

While it's miles possible to run any kind of proprietary protocol on top of TCP/

IP, there are some popular and extensively supported standard protocols. If

You operate a wellknown protocol to deliver your sensor facts, you'll be capable of

Paintings with many extra devices and packages than in case you developed your

Very own proprietary protocol.

The most important preferred protocol through a long way is the Hypertext transfer

Protocol (HTTP), the protocol of the arena wide web. HTTP describes

How a purchaser interacts with a server, by means of sending request messages and

Message

Web browsers are the most famous HTTP customers, but you can without difficulty

Write your personal customers—and your own servers. In case you use an internet browser to

Get right of entry to a device, the device has the position of a web server, supplying an internet

Service over the net.

A server incorporates assets, which may be some thing of hobby, e.G., a Document (commonly an HTML web page), the maximum contemporary dimension of a sensor, or the configuration of a tool. Whilst you design a

Net carrier, you want to decide which sources it need to disclose to The world.

HTTP makes use of Uniform useful resource Identifiers (URIs) to inform the server which

Useful resource the consumer wants to read, write, create, or delete. You already know URIs

From net surfing; they appearance something like these:1

Optionally, a URI may additionally comprise a query (e.G., alarm=excessive) after a ?
Person that follows the direction.

For the HTTP protocol, port eighty is utilized by default except any other port is

Selected explicitly, possibly for testing purposes. The path is referred to as request

URI in HTTP; it denotes the target useful resource of an HTTP request.

Be aware: URIs that start with a scheme are absolute URIs. URIs with out a

Scheme are relative URIs. A request URI is a relative URI that begins with /.

Occasionally you'll must paintings with absolute URIs and different times with Relative URIs, as you may see in the examples.

There are numerous styles of HTTP requests that a customer can send, but the

Most popular are GET for analyzing a useful resource, put for writing to a resource,

Submit for developing a useful resource, and DELETE for deleting a useful resource. Web

Browsers broadly speaking trouble GET requests, which make up the vast majority of

HTTP requests. In a web of factors software, a GET request to a URI,

Positioned requests, post requests, and GET responses deliver representations

Of the addressed useful resource. The first-class-known representation is the Hypertext Markup Language, higher known as HTML. An internet browser is an HTTP

Purchaser that knows a way to render HTML pages at the display screen. There are different

Popular representations: PDF, JPEG, XML-based totally statistics formats, and so on. A web

Service may also support one or numerous representations for a unmarried resource.

You know the hypertext links from HTML, which use URIs to address

Different resources. By way of clicking on a hyperlink, you motive the browser to ship a

GET request to reap a representation of that aid. This request is

Despatched to the host contained in the link's URI.

Let's look at a whole example of an HTTP request/response interplay

1. This diagram shows a GET request, as it is able to be sent with the aid of an internet browser

Or your very own purchaser program. The patron requests a illustration of the

Useful resource's "real temperature as measured via the temperature sensor,"

Whose URI consists of the host www.Example.Com and the request URI

/temperatures/actual.

2. The provider at host www.Instance.Com gets the request, measures

The temperature, and returns a response message. In this case

Even the maximum complex net interactions encompass such message

Exchanges. The web consists of several hundred million customers and numerous

Hundred thousand servers with their resources, and it produces a torrent

Of messages that convey aid representations. The technical term

For this structure is representational state switch, or rest.

The point of interest of having began with the internet of things is to expose how

Rest and not unusual web standards can be used as the desired manner of

Growing net of factors applications. Such applications are sometimes

Known as internet of factors programs, to emphasize using internet standards

On pinnacle of the simple net protocols.

The web of things consists of RESTful internet offerings that measure or

Control bodily houses.

For this reason, the time period web of factors focuses on the utility layer and the

Actual-world "things" which are measured or manipulated. The time period internet

Of factors makes a speciality of the underlying network layers and the technical

Way for measuring and manipulating the physical environment— i.E.,

Sensors and actuators.

Push as opposed to Pull

There are 4 basic ways in which your device might also speak with

Every other computer at the web:

1. Tool is the patron, pushing records to a server

2. Device is the customer, pulling facts from a server

Three. Tool is the server, presenting data to clients

Four. Device is the server, accepting data from clients

Those styles can be visualized as proven in parent four-5. A black arrow

Shows the course of a request message and a dotted arrow shows

The direction wherein records flows, i.E., wherein direction a aid Illustration is sent.

PRIMARY NET INTERACTION PATTERNS

In monitoring packages, a device produces information, i.E., measurements

From its connected sensors. For such packages, the interplay patterns

1 and three are suitable: information flows from the tool to any other computer; the

Tool is either consumer (1) or server (3).

In control packages, a device consumes facts, i.E., commands from

A web browser or other patron. For such programs, the interplay

Patterns 2 and four are appropriate: information flows to the tool from another

Laptop; the device is either consumer (2) or server (4).

Observe: a web browser is a purchaser that mainly pulls records from internet servers

Through sending GET requests to them. So you are in all likelihood maximum familiar with

Interplay sample 2 because this is the way web browsers paintings.

In part II, i can focus at the device as patron (i.E., on eventualities 1 and a couple of).

Considering the fact that in general, a device cannot realize in advance when you want to send

It a command (e.G., to set up an actuator or to reconfigure a sensor), it

Makes sense to aid gadgets as servers as well. Therefore, i can talk

Scenarios 3 and four in component III. I trust that the capacity of the internet of

Things will best be realized if gadgets can come to be clients, servers, or each.

After each size, the Netduino Plus straight away

Sends the sample to a server for garage and later retrieval. This server

Effectively provides a feed aid to which you post your data

Samples. You may already recognise the concept of feeds from RSS feed

Readers. A feed entry may be some thing of interest, from political information to

Blog entries to measurements, as in the case of your Netduino Plus. In

A manner, a feed that includes measurements can be concept of as a news

Source approximately the physical global.

For such an example, you want a appropriate internet provider to which your

Tool can send its measurements. Quite simply, there's a free service,

Pachube, which does exactly this. It presents web-based totally interfaces for

Storing and for getting access to feeds, as proven in parent five-1.

note: the instance in determine five-1 is a NASA feed.

To use Pachube, you need a unfastened account and a feed to which you may

Ship your very own facts. Follow those steps to create each the account and a

First feed:

Be aware: Your Netduino Plus packages will send the API key along side

Every HTTP request to Pachube. The API key tells Pachube that your

Patron program is allowed to feature new measurements for your feeds

The place itself (click on on the Google map to define the place). In case you

Pick out to provide a region, I advise you pick a famous public point

Of interest close to you as opposed to your actual domestic deal with.

11. Note the id of this feed. It's far a part of the net web page URI (circled in

Parent 5-2).

Determine five-2. Enhancing the houses of a Pachube feed

observe: A Pachube feed incorporates one or numerous statistics streams; for instance,

A feed may also contain one information movement for each sensor in a building. Inside the

Handiest case, a feed has only one records circulate—for the measurements of

One sensor. In our examples, we can use records streams: one for voltage

Values, the other for easy integer numbers.

Forty Getting began with the net of factors

12.Click on on "+ upload a brand new datastream". Enter "voltage" because the identity, enter

"Volt" within the gadgets subject, and input V in the image subject. In type, select

"derived SI", which means that this is a unit derived from some different

Physical devices which can be considered extra simple.

13. Click on "+ upload a new datastream" again. Input "range" because the id and

Leave all other houses as they're.

14. Click on save Feed.

15. Given your Pachube feed id, observe the feed's domestic web page by using typing in its

JSON

JSON, which stands for JavaScript item Notation, is a textual

Format for representing arbitrary statistics. In this recognize, it is similar

To the regularly-used XML illustration. JSON is popular for internet

Applications considering that its text is less complicated and generally much less verbose

Than equal XML textual content. At the same time as JSON is a part of the JavaScript

Language, it is supported with the aid of libraries for almost all programming languages today, and has thereby gained "a life of its own."

Right here is an example of JSON textual content:

 The consumer, through His internet browser, sends HTTP GET requests to Pachube to retrieve feed

Entries. The statistics glide originates inside the device, is going up to Pachube, and Continues from there to the person.

this means that you have a nearby location network to

Which both the board and your development computer are connected. All through

Development and debugging, the laptop and Netduino Plus are directly Linked through a USB cable as well.

INTERNET ADDRESSES

A router typically implements the Dynamic Host Configuration

Protocol (DHCP). This protocol lets in your improvement laptop, your

Netduino Plus, and different gadgets to mechanically reap internet The net protocols rely on net addresses for Routing messages between customers and servers.

Wherein xxx lies among 0 and 255. Public net servers never use

These reserved addresses. They're unique best inside a given neighborhood region

Community, no longer international like other net addresses.

To implement one of these multiplexing of net addresses, a router has

To perform community cope with translation (NAT). This hides the non-public

Internet addresses from the net by using making it appear as though all

Net visitors from the board or from the improvement pc originated

From the router. This offers a positive degree of safety due to the fact a

Software at the internet cannot at once cope with—and therefore try to

Connect with—a device hidden in the back of the router.

On account that such internet addresses are not very handy,

You could as an alternative use a site call for addressing a number. Inside the

Above instance, the domain name is pachube.Com. Domains are

Registered with the net's area call gadget (DNS). The domain Name device permits for looking up domain names, lots within the same way

As a cellphone book is used for looking up names (besides instead of locating

Smartphone numbers, the domain call machine returns internet addresses).

The MFDeploy tool

Earlier than you may use your Netduino Plus on the community, you want to test

Its network settings and configure it if vital. Specially, you must

Make certain that DHCP is switched on and that the proper MAC address of

The board is about.

To check or modify the network configuration, use the tool MFDeploy,

Which is supplied as a part of the Microsoft .Net Micro Framework SDK.

Now, perform the subsequent steps:

1. Begin MFDeploy.Exe. The dialog field .Net Micro Framework Deployment

Device opens.

2. Inside the leftmost device list container, exchange the choice from Serial to USB.

3. Plug your Netduino Plus USB cable into your development pc. Inside the

Rightmost device listing container, the call NetduinoPlus_NetduinoPlus must

Seem.

4. Click at the Ping button to make sure the tool responds. As result, the

Big text field should now display "Pinging... TinyCLR".

Five. Within the target menu, select Configuration→community. The community

Configuration conversation field opens.

6. If it is not checked already, click at the DHCP checkbox to enable automatic configuration of maximum community parameters.

7. If it isn't configured yet, input your board's MAC deal with. That is the simplest
8. Click the update button.
9. Reboot your Netduino Plus. It need to now routinely attain the missing network parameters from your router. To make sure that the Netduino

Plus reboots, I normally perform a whole power-off/strength-on cycle by using

In short unplugging and reinserting the USB cable from the computer. After such

A strength cycle, you have got five seconds to deploy a brand new software; in any other case,

The maximum lately deployed program is restarted automatically.

Community Configuration in MFDeploy

To check whether or not the configuration works efficiently, run the HelloPachube
Client application described subsequent.

```
const string apiKey = "your Pachube API key";
const string feedId = "your Pachube feed id";
const int samplingPeriod = 20000; // 20 seconds
const double maxVoltage = three.Three;
const int maxAdcValue = 1023;
var voltagePort = new AnalogInput(Pins.GPIO_PIN_A1);
var lowPort = new OutputPort(Pins.GPIO_PIN_A0, fake);
var highPort = new OutputPort(Pins.GPIO_PIN_A2, genuine);
at the same time as (real)

  WaitUntilNextPeriod(samplingPeriod);
int rawValue = voltagePort.Read();
double price = (rawValue * maxVoltage) / maxAdcValue;
string pattern = "voltage," + price.ToString("f");
  Debug.Print("new message: " + pattern);
  PachubeClient.Ship(apiKey, feedId, sample);


long now = DateTime.Now.Ticks / TimeSpan.TicksPerMillisecond;
var offset = (int)(now % period);
int postpone = length - offset;
  Debug.Print("sleep for " + put off + " msrn");
  Thread.Sleep(put off);
```

To run this system, comply with those steps:

1. Ensure that your Netduino Plus is connected in your Ethernet

Router and that it is correctly configured for community get entry to (see the

Preceding phase).

2. If you haven't completed so already, download the visual Studio assignment Gsiot.

PachubeClient from http://www.Gsiot.Info/down load/, unzip it, and put

It into the visual Studio 2010Projects directory.

3. Create a brand new visual Studio project (the use of the Netduino Plus template) And name it HelloPachube.

4. You ought to replace the strings for apiKey and feedId so that they healthy your

Pachube API key and feed identification.

5. Proper-click on on References in the answer Explorer. Choose upload→

New Reference. Within the upload Reference dialog container, click on on the Browse tab.

Inside the directory hierarchy, go up two steps to listing mission. Within the

Directory Gsiot.PachubeClient, open the subdirectory Gsiot.PachubeClient (yes, the equal call once more). On this listing, open the bin subdirectory. From there, open the discharge subdirectory. On this subdirectory,

Choose the Gsiot.PachubeClient.Dll record. Click the adequate button.

observe: in the handiest case, one C# namespace is translated into precisely

One .Net assembly (stored in a DLL), which is the binary form of .Internet code.

For the .Internet Micro Framework, a integrated postprocessor device translates .Dll

Meeting documents into .Pe documents, that are a more compact representation of

The same code. These are the documents that get deployed to the Netduino Plus.

Viewing the results

After HelloPachube has commenced, you'll see some thing just like the following in

Visible Studio's Output window:

Sleep for 19069 ms

The thread '<No Name>' (0x3) has exited with code zero (0x0).

To verify that the samples have certainly arrived at Pachube, type the subsequent URI into your web browser, changing your Pachube feed id with

Your feed identity:

Http://www.Pachube.Com/feeds/your   Pachube   feed identification

You should now see that the fame of your feed is marked as presently:

Stay. Which means the most current pattern isn't older than 15 mins;

In any other case, the reputation currently: frozen could be shown.

Notice: if you don't see this output, make certain that the Netduino Plus

Is hooked up via Ethernet cable to a router, and via USB cable on your

Development computer. Use MFDeploy to check whether or not DHCP is enabled and

The MAC address is set. Take a look at whether the example effectively builds and

Whether or not its houses are set up to install to the device through USB.

To peer a graphical illustration of the most recent samples, view the

Feed's internet web page, study the graph there, and click the label "remaining hour".

How it Works

The initialization of the HelloPachube main approach begins with

Pachube-related constants: your Pachube API key (apiKey) and the identification of

The feed to which you need to post your samples (feedId). After that,

There are some other constants and variables which might be set:

» Specifying how regularly to ship updates

First comes the timing-related steady samplingPeriod. The goal for

The instance is to pattern and post a brand new remark at ordinary intervals, specifically as soon as every samplingPeriod, which is given in milliseconds

(20,000 milliseconds is 20 seconds).

To submit a pattern, ship an internet request and await its

response. The

Time for one of these entire spherical-journey consists of the time it takes for the

Request to tour to the server, for the server to create a reaction, and For the reaction to travel lower back to the patron.

observe: the velocity of the round-journey depends mainly on 5 elements: the

Distance between customer and server, the modern traffic at the internet,

The overall performance of the server, the current load of the server, and the

Amount of statistics transferred. Typical numbers variety from approximately 50 milliseconds for round-journeys to servers near the customer, to properly over 1,000

Milliseconds for spherical-trips across continents or to overtaxed servers

(even for short messages). In view that they rely upon the internet's contemporary

Site visitors, the times for subsequent round-journeys from the equal purchaser to the

Identical server can vary.

If you use a slower connection than Ethernet, this may additionally affect roundtrip instances. For instance, in case you dropped a Netduino out in the woods with a

Reasonably-priced 2G GSM module, it would likely spend maximum of the 20 seconds

Doing the round-experience.

» setting up the voltage reader

The voltagePort object and related variables and constants are set up,

As you saw in chapter 3. They're used for studying voltage values from An attached potentiometer.

The main loop does basically 3 matters:

» Sleeps until the following pattern is due, the usage of the helper approach WaitUntilNextPeriod, which i can discuss within the subsequent segment.

» Creates the sample by using studying the voltage port.

» Sends the cost to Pachube using PachubeClient.Ship. This technique

Takes the Pachube API key, your feed identity, plus the pattern information, and

Sends them to Pachube in a appropriate positioned request message. It then

Gets the reaction message and prints the response's popularity code To the debug console.

To apply the Gsiot.PachubeClient for sending requests to Pachube in a

"hearth and overlook" manner, you don't need to recognize more than this. However,

If you need to understand how the library in reality works, how you may adjust.

PERIOD TECHNIQUE

In this example, samples ought to be taken at pretty normal durations. To do

This, you could use the WaitUntilNextPeriod helper approach, which you could

Reuse in similar packages later on. The subsequent text explains the approach

In a few detail. You could pass the rationale in case you just need to move in advance

And use the approach.

After every pattern is despatched, the program wishes to sleep until the next

Duration begins. How can this postpone be calculated with precision when we

Don't understand earlier precisely how long it'll take to ship a request and

Receive its response?

This example begins a new length every 20 seconds. (loose Pachube

Debts don't allow updates extra frequently than every 12 seconds.)

Count on the following:

» You remaining took a reading at 09:32:forty.

» After the time it took you to ship a message and acquire the reaction,

It is now 09:32:46.

» You want to send the next message (and start a brand new length) at

09:33:00.

The postpone then can be calculated because the distinction among the duration of

The length (20 seconds) and the offset, in which the offset shows how

Some distance you are into the contemporary duration. The offset is calculated because the modern

Time (i.E., now) modulo the duration. In the example proven in parent 6-four,

The offset is six seconds; consequently, the postpone is 14 seconds.

Fifty four Getting commenced with the internet of things

Discern 6-4. Calculating the delay until the begin of the subsequent length

The property DateTime.Now.Ticks gives the current time3 in ticks, which in

.Net is a time at a decision of a hundred nanoseconds. Dividing ticks through 10,000

(TimeSpan.TicksPerMillisecond) yields the equal time in milliseconds,

Albeit much less precisely. This calls for a 64-bit lengthy integer type.

To calculate The modulus, use the % operator of C#. Because the end result of a modulus

Operation is constantly smaller than the operand, in this example length, it can be

Correctly forged to a 32-bit integer the use of the (int) solid.

Notice: The modulo operator, %, computes the the rest of a division.

For example, the department of seven by 2 yields three. Computing "backwards" by means of

Multiplying the result 3 through the divisor 2, we get 6. The difference among

6 and the dividend (7) is the remainder—in this case, 1.

WaitUntilNextPeriod ensures that sampling begins at exceptionally normal

Intervals. It's far strong even in instances in which an new release takes longer than

Its duration lets in for. This could occur if something unexpected takes place,

Inclusive of an exception that takes an inordinately long time to be despatched to the

Debugger. This may result in one or several durations being skipped—however

The following one starts offevolved at a accurate length boundary anyway.

Three On a Netduino, this is the time because the tool has booted. It has no battery-backed real-time clock that

Maintains music of time whilst it isn't powered.

Casting Values

C# gives numerous integer sorts, which differ in the variety tiers

That they embody and inside the bits used for storing them.

Any int variable i suits in a long Variable l, so the challenge l = i constantly works. But, the opposite

Direction does now not continually paintings: most long numbers do no longer match in an int

Variable. Consequently, C# requires the use of a kind solid, i = (int)l, to make it

Apparent that this danger exists right here. If l is too large whilst it's miles assigned

To i, i could be assigned rubbish. So when the compiler requires any such Kind forged, it is a great concept to consider whether you could absolutely make sure That the current value of l fits into i.

An HTTP request includes one request line, accompanied by using quite a number

Of header strains, observed via an empty line, and optionally observed by way of a

Message frame (i.E., the message's content material).

The request line starts with the HTTP method: put, GET, and so forth. After a

Clean, the request URI shows the useful resource to be accessed. After

Any other clean, the HTTP version is given, which is typically model 1.1

Nowadays. The request line is terminated via a carriage-return byte Observed via a newline byte.

 If you have been to look at the real text of the request,

They might not be seen.

HTTP defines a number of headers, each for requests and responses. For

Requests, the Host header is specifically vital because it defines to

Which laptop the request is despatched—in this example, to

api.Pachube.Com. In case you

Take this host and the request URI in the request line (right here, it's /v2/feeds/

Fid.Csv)

Unlike the URIs that we have visible in chapter 5, which have been URIs

For purchasers of Pachube feeds, that is a URI for producers that send

Measurements to Pachube.

Distinctive programs may additionally use very special units of headers. For our

Functions, the most vital headers are Host (for requests most effective) and

Content material-duration and content-kind (for both requests and responses).

Note: To discover what exactly your customer is sending, you may use a

Easy take a look at server (this kind of server is given in Appendix A). To make HelloPachube send its requests to a check server walking in your laptop, alternate the

Steady baseUri in Gsiot.PachubeClient so that it points to your server.

In this reaction, the first line, known as the fame line, is the maximum

Vital. HTTP defines some of status codes; repute code two hundred

Means that the request was treated successfully.The reputation code is located

Between the HTTP model and a simple-textual content version of the popularity code.

The textual content version of the status code is optionally available—you neither want to

Generate nor interpret it. It's miles merely a convenience for human readers

Of HTTP interactions.

Responses may contain many headers, as you could see from this situation.

Fortunately, you could usually forget about nearly all of them. Despite the fact that, let's

Take a look at the headers inside the response:

» Server

Suggests the web server software program that Pachube makes use of.

» Date

Suggests the time when Pachube has despatched the reaction.

» content material-type: textual content/simple; charset=utf-eight

Suggests the layout of the Pachube reaction. In this example, it's miles plain textual content

Encoded in UTF8 (the most common encoding of Unicode characters).

58 Getting started out with the internet of factors

observe: truly, with many web services, the reaction to a successful

Positioned request has an empty message body. The server is allowed to go back

A response frame, though.

» Connection: hold-alive

Is a relic from HTTP 1.0 (an early version of the HTTP specification).

In the beginning, a new TCP/IP connection changed into opened for every request and

Then closed after the request. Due to the fact starting a connection incurs a

Sizable overhead, it's miles better to hold a connection open if requests

Are sent to the equal server every couple of seconds. The hold-alive

Cost was added to suggest this preference. It is not applicable anymore because maximum servers and customers these days aid HTTP 1.1, wherein

Connections are saved alive by default. However, if for any motive a purchaser

Or a server wants to near a connection after a message trade, it is able to

Sign this to the other celebration by using along with the relationship: close header.

Observe: A connection can also be closed even whilst request or reaction

Messages are being exchanged—e.G., if a person tripped over your

Ethernet cable and it changed into yanked out. Which means that closed

Connections need to be reopened if important, lost messages may have

To be re-despatched, and clients and servers must be programmed in a manner

That they do not misbehave—although a connection is closed.

» Set-Cookie

Shows a cookie (some text that the server sends a patron to shop, and

Which the customer will ship to the server in destiny requests) with a consultation

Identifier. You could ignore cookies due to the fact they're now not needed for our

Examples.

» Cache-manage: max-age=zero

Is supposed for handling caches among client and server. It suggests

That this response ought to not be cached.

» content material-period: 1

Shows that the response message frame includes one byte.

» Age: zero

Is an estimate (in seconds) of the time it has taken to produce and

Transmit the reaction. It's miles a header produced through a few middleman Cache among server and patron. You can ignore it.

» vary: receive-Encoding

Tells the customer that it could send an take delivery of-Encoding header along

With GET requests, for you to ask for one-of-a-kind representations of the

Useful resource.

It seems a bit ordinary that it is not absolutely empty

In the case of Pachube, however you can normally forget about the message body of a

Placed reaction besides.

HTTP requests and responses aren't complicated. Any tool capable of

Assisting TCP/IP is capable of ship information to Pachube or to similar services.

REQUESTS THE SIMPLE MANNER

It Completely hides the .Internet classes needed to enforce an HTTP client. If

You want to use Pachube in a special way, or in case you need to write clients for

Different offerings, you can use the greater popular HttpWebRequest and HttpWebResponse classes, which might be positioned within the device.Net namespace.

SimplePutRequest

Instance 7-1 suggests how these instructions can be used to ship a single sample

To Pachube.

Example 7-1. SimplePutRequest

The usage of machine.IO;

Using gadget.Internet;

The usage of device.Text;

The use of Microsoft.SPOT;

Public class SimplePutRequest

public static void predominant()

const string apiKey = "your Pachube API key";
const string feedId = "your Pachube feed identity";

```
// this is the "pattern" we want to ship to Pachube
var sample = "wide variety,forty two";
// convert sample to byte array

 byte[] buffer = Encoding.UTF8.GetBytes(pattern);
// produce request
var requestUri =
"http://api.Pachube.Com/v2/feeds/" + feedId + ".Csv";
the use of (var request = (HttpWebRequest)WebRequest.
Create(requestUri))

 request.Technique = "placed";
// headers
request.ContentType = "textual content/csv";
request.ContentLength = buffer.Length;
request.Headers.Upload("X-PachubeApiKey", apiKey);
// content material
movement s = request.GetRequestStream(); s.Write(buffer, zero,
buffer.Duration);
// ship request and get hold of reaction
using (var response = (HttpWebResponse)request.
 GetResponse())

// consume response
 Debug.Print("fame code: " + reaction.StatusCode);
```

To run this situation:

1. Ensure your Netduino Plus is hooked up for your Ethernet

router, and

That it is efficaciously configured for community get right of entry to (see chapter 6).

2. Create a new visual Studio mission (the usage of the Netduino Plus template)

And call it SimplePutRequest. Replace the contents of program.Cs with

The code from instance 7-1.

3. You should update the strings for apiKey and feedId in order that they suit

Your Pachube API key and feed identification.

4. Proper-click on References within the solution Explorer. Pick out upload→New Reference. In the add Reference dialog field, click on on the .Internet tab (if it is not

Already decided on). Discover device.Http inside the listing and click on good enough to add this

Assembly on your undertaking.

C# "the use of" Statements

Both HttpWebRequest and HttpWebResponse put into effect the

IDisposable interface, which means that they provide Dispose

Strategies. Times of such kinds ought to be disposed once they

Were created and used by calling their Dispose techniques.

(if you fail to create the object for some motive, Dispose can't

And need not be known as.)

To prevent you from having to address this in your very own, C# presents

The the usage of announcement, which routinely calls Dispose at the end of

The code block, even though an exception came about:

Using (var request = (HttpWebRequest)WebRequest.

Create(requestUri))

// set up request line parameters, headers, and content material

using (var reaction =

(HttpWebResponse)request.GetResponse())

// eat reaction

Now, you're equipped to test it: build the undertaking and deploy it on your Netduino

Plus, as defined within the segment "Deploying to the device" in chapter 1.

A dummy "pattern" is then defined and transformed from a string to a byte

Array with a call to Encoding.UTF8.GetBytes. (while you want to transform

Inside the different route, use Encoding.UTF8.GetChars to achieve a individual

Array, and then name new string(charArray).)

While you look at your Pachube feed web page, you'll notice that on the

Backside of the page, statistics flow range has now appeared below information

Stream voltage.

Sixty four Getting began with the internet of things

Making net Requests

SimplePutRequest makes use of 3 lessons from Microsoft's gadget.Internet

Namespace: WebRequest,   HttpWebRequest,   and HttpWebResponse:

» WebRequest

A manufacturing facility elegance (a category that generates different instructions) whose method

WebRequest.Create(requestUriString) creates an object that

Represents a request for the protocol indicated by using the argument

RequestUriString. It troubles a DNS research to discover the net

Deal with of the area call given in the requestUriString.

Alternatively, it accepts URIs that immediately incorporate net addresses

In place of domains.

» HttpWebRequest

A complete HTTP request with its headers and body.

» HttpWebResponse

A whole HTTP response with its headers and body.

Those training are applied in the system.Http meeting, imparting

Help for clients of net services. While used, you need to reference

Them in your visible Studio assignment.

Word: system.Http is a huge meeting, taking over about -thirds of the

Flash reminiscence to be had in your utility code (on a Netduino Plus

With the standard firmware), or kind of 46 KB.

THE HTTP WEB REQUEST CLASS

The approach WebRequest.Create takes a URI string as a controversy and

Creates a new object of type WebRequest. If the URI begins with http, the

Object it returns is a subclass of WebRequest, namely an HttpWebRequest.

This means that a kind solid can be used:

Var request = (HttpWebRequest)WebRequest.Create(requestUri);

An HttpWebRequest object has numerous houses that correspond to

Elements of an HTTP request line or to a few crucial HTTP headers.

You need to set the following ones earlier than you are making the request:

» The method assets (in the instance above, request.Technique) represents post, or DELETE. This fee may be despatched as part of the HTTP request line, which is The first line of an HTTP request.

» You have to initialize the ContentLength assets with the duration of the

Request message body in bytes (now not counting the request line and the

Request headers). This fee will be despatched as the content material-duration header

Of the request message.

» You must initialize the ContentType property with a string indicating

The kind of content you'll be sending. In instance 7-1, this turned into text/csv,

Which suggests you'll be sending comma-separated values. This cost

Might be sent as the content-type header of the request message.

» Pachube requires that you authorize new samples via presenting the

X-PachubeApiKey header with your API key. Without a legitimate API key,

Pachube does not take delivery of new samples from a client. Due to the fact that is a

Nonstandard HTTP header, the method Headers.Upload is used for adding

It to the request item.

You furthermore mght want to put in writing the HTTP body to a byte flow, which has been

Created along with the request object. You'll achieve it by using calling the

Request's GetRequestStream approach. After writing the whole contents of

The byte buffer that contains your pattern into this flow, you need to shut

The flow. Luckily, the using statement does this robotically.

Word: As for the connection control, it occurs in the back of the

Scenes—i.E., HttpWebRequest.GetResponse automatically reuses an

Open connection to the host if one is to be had; otherwise, it creates

A brand new connection. It continues this connection open unless you have set

Request.KeepAlive to false, which units the relationship header to close

In preference to the (redundant) maintain-alive. If the response message contains A Connection: near header, the connection is closed as nicely.

ISBN: 9798823841900